Confidence

Ashley Lee

Explore other books at:
WWW.ENGAGEBOOKS.COM

VANCOUVER, B.C.

e WWW.ENGAGEBOOKS.COM

Confidence: Good Character Traits
Lee, Ashley, 1995 –
Text © 2024 Engage Books
Design © 2024 Engage Books

Edited by: A.R. Roumanis
Design by: Mandy Christiansen

Text set in Myriad Pro Regular.
Chapter headings set in Anton.

FIRST EDITION / FIRST PRINTING

All rights reserved. No part of this book may be stored in a retrieval system, reproduced or transmitted in any form or by any other means without written permission from the publisher or a licence from the Canadian Copyright Licensing Agency. Critics and reviewers may quote brief passages in connection with a review or critical article in any media.

Every reasonable effort has been made to contact the copyright holders of all material reproduced in this book.

LIBRARY AND ARCHIVES CANADA CATALOGUING IN PUBLICATION

Title: Confidence / Ashley Lee.
Names: Lee, Ashley, author.
Description: Series statement: Good Character Traits

Identifiers: Canadiana (print) 20230446973 | Canadiana (ebook) 20230446981
ISBN 978-1-77878-647-1 (hardcover)
ISBN 978-1-77878-648-8 (softcover)
ISBN 978-1-77878-649-5 (epub)
ISBN 978-1-77878-650-1 (pdf)

This project has been made possible in part by the Government of Canada.

Canada

Confidence

Contents

4   What Is Confidence?
6   Why Is Confidence Important?
8   What Does Confidence Look Like?
10 How Does Confidence Affect You?
12 How Does Confidence Affect Others?
14 Is Everyone Confident?
16 Is It Bad if You Are Not Confident?
18 Does Confidence Change Over Time?
20 Is It Hard to Be Confident?
22 How Can You Learn to Be More Confident?
24 How Can You Help Others Be More Confident?
26 How to Be Confident Every Day
28 Confidence Around the World
30 Quiz

What Is Confidence?

Confidence is when you believe in yourself.

Confidence

It means you know you can do something.

Why Is Confidence Important?

Confidence helps you feel happy.

Confidence

It helps you try new things.

What Does Confidence Look Like?

Confident people stand tall. They speak with a strong voice.

Confidence

They are not **afraid** to tell other people their ideas.

Key Word
Afraid: scared.

How Does Confidence Affect You?

Confidence makes you feel good about yourself.

Confidence

It helps you be strong when things are hard.

How Does Confidence Affect Others?

Being confident can make other people feel confident too.

Confidence

Let others see you try something new. People will know it is okay to try new things too.

Is Everyone Confident?

Sometimes people are not confident. That is okay.

14

Confidence

Sometimes people are confident with some things but not others.

Is It Bad if You Are Not Confident?

It is not bad if you are not confident.

Confidence

It just means you have not learned how great you are.

17

Does Confidence Change Over Time?

Confidence can go up or down over time.

Confidence

Your confidence about something often goes up the more you do it.

Is It Hard to Be Confident?

It can take a lot of hard work to become confident.

Confidence

Practicing something can help you feel more confident about it.

Key Word

Practicing: doing something over and over again so you get better at it.

How Can You Learn to Be More Confident?

Think about all the things you are good at.

Confidence

Learn from your **mistakes**.

> **Key Word**
>
> **Mistakes:** things that people did wrong.

How Can You Help Others Be More Confident?

Tell your friends you are happy for them when they do well.

Confidence

Encourage your friends to try new things.

Key Word

Encourage: say or do things to help other people keep trying.

How to Be Confident Every Day

1. Celebrate when you do something well.
2. Try new things.

Key Word

Celebrate: do something fun for a special event.

Confidence

3. Think happy thoughts.

4. Do not put yourself down.

Confidence Around the World

People all over the world make choices every day. You need confidence to do this.

Confidence

You need to believe that you will make the right choice.

Quiz

Test your knowledge of confidence by answering the following questions. The questions are based on what you have read in this book. The answers are listed on the bottom of the next page.

1 Does confidence help you feel happy?

2 Are confident people afraid to tell other people their ideas?

3 Can being confident make other people feel confident too?

4 Is it bad if you are not confident?

5 Can confidence go up or down over time?

6 Should you put yourself down?

30

Explore Other Pre-1 Readers.

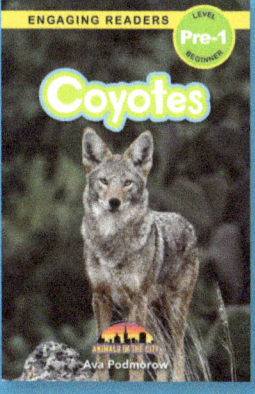

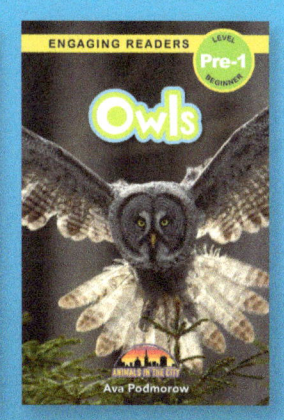

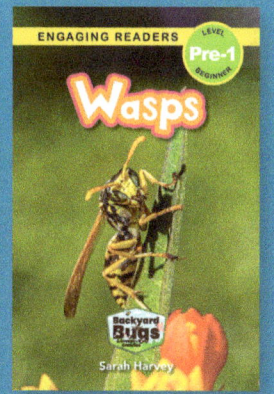

Visit www.engagebooks.com/readers

Answers: 1. Yes 2. No 3. Yes 4. No 5. Yes 6. No

Milton Keynes UK
Ingram Content Group UK Ltd.
UKHW051111221024
450084UK00017B/181